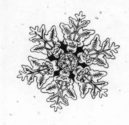

Christmas

ISSUE

ideals

∗

edited and prepared
by van b. hooper

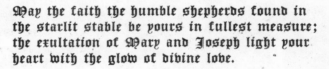

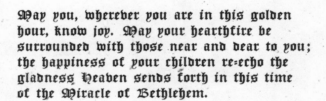

May you, wherever you are in this golden
hour, know joy. May your hearthfire be
surrounded with those near and dear to you;
the happiness of your children re-echo the
gladness Heaven sends forth in this time
of the Miracle of Bethlehem.

May the faith the humble shepherds found in
the starlit stable be yours in fullest measure;
the exultation of Mary and Joseph light your
heart with the glow of divine love.

May you gather together in bright bouquet
love, charity and tranquillity of spirit, for
he who possesses these holds the key to
riches beyond measure.

May all your dreams in this splendid hour
reach fulfillment, and may all the paths you
walk be lighted with peace, not only today,
but in all the days of the year to come.

© *Loretta Bauer Buckley*

IDEALS — Vol. 14, No. 5 — October, 1957. Published Quarterly by Ideals Publishing Co., 3510 W. St. Paul Ave., Milwaukee 1, Wis. Entered as second class matter February 17, 1949, at the Post Office at Milwaukee, Wis., under Act of Congress, March 3, 1879. Copyright © 1957 by Ideals Publishing Co. All rights reserved. Title **IDEALS** registered U.S. Patent Office.

ONE YEAR SUBSCRIPTION — four consecutive issues as published — only $5.00. TWO YEAR SUBSCRIPTION — eight consecutive issues as published — only $10.00. SINGLE ISSUES $1.50 per copy. The cover and entire contents of IDEALS are fully protected by copyright and must not be reproduced in any manner whatsoever. Printed and bound in U. S. A.

A Little Bit Of Christmas

Garnett Ann Schultz

Just a little bit of Christmas
　　and the whole world seems to glow
With a special sort of laughter
　　that we love and treasure so —
Nothing more than just some holly
　　or a wreath upon the door
And it fills our hearts with Christmas
　　and the season we adore.

Just a little bit of giving
　　and we know a warmth and pride,
There's a feeling of contentment,
　　ever growing deep inside —
It is such a pleasant custom
　　as we tie each package bright
And however small the present,
　　it's the thought that brings delight.

Just a little bit of praying
   and how very sure we are
That we've found God ever loving,
   and we've seen that wondrous star.
There are angel voices singing
   and their music fills the air
With a little bit of Christmas
   being scattered everywhere.

Just a little bit of knowing
   of the meaning of this day
And a little real believing
   in the words we kneel and pray,
Just a little bit of sharing,
   all the faith it might impart
Just a little bit of Christmas
   puts a peace in every heart.

©

Though time crumbles stone,
and the Story grows old,
Yet the Shepherd we love
still watches His fold;
And His star still shines
over city and mart,
And His voice still speaks
to the listening heart.

Pamela Vaull Starr
©

The Christmas Story

Throughout the ages — the Story of the Birth of Christ has been an inspiration to artists in all walks of life. Old masters from the far corners of the world — contemporary artists — actors — sculptors — artisans alike have strived to express this story in their own way.

For your pleasure we present on the following pages a wide variety of expressions of the Greatest Story ever told.

Editor

My Prayer

Annette Victorin

Please help me Lord, to cherish sacred things:
Help me to keep a child's deep trust in me,
Teach me to listen when a robin sings,
To watch a spider weave its artistry.

Give me the keys that will unlock the hearts
Of all I meet; please help me understand
Ways not my own that fill their daily charts,
Encourage me to offer them my hand.

Show me the grace of sparrows in the snow,
Help me to teach my children gold is cold,
That what can be replaced has little glow
And only gentle deeds wear well when old;

Remind me, Peace will be a dream come true,
When men follow the Star that leads to You.

©

How the Great Guest Came

Edwin Markham

Before the cathedral in grandeur rose
At Ingelburg where the Danube goes;
Before its forest of silver spires
Went airily up to the clouds and fires;
Before the oak had ready a beam,
While yet the arch was stone and dream —
There where the altar was later laid,
Conrad, the cobbler, plied his trade.

It happened one day at the year's white end —
Two neighbors called on their old-time friend;
And they found the shop, so meager and mean,
Made gay with a hundred boughs of green.
Conrad was stitching with face ashine,
But suddenly stopped as he twitched a twine:
"Old friends, good news! At dawn today,
As the cocks were scaring the night away,
The Lord appeared in a dream to me,
And said, 'I am coming your Guest to be!'
So I've been busy with feet astir,
Strewing the floor with branches of fir.
The wall is washed and the shelf is shined,
And over the rafter the holly twined.
He comes today, and the table is spread
With milk and honey and wheaten bread."

His friends went home; and his face grew still
As he watched for the shadow across the sill.
He lived all the moments o'er and o'er,
When the Lord should enter the lowly door—
The knock, the call, the latch pulled up,
The lighted face, the offered cup.
He would wash the feet where the spikes had been,
He would kiss the hands where the nails went in,
And then at the last would sit with Him
And break the bread as the day grew dim.

While the cobbler mused there passed his pane
A beggar drenched by the driving rain.
He called him in from the stony street
And gave him shoes for his bruised feet.
The beggar went and there came a crone,
Her face with wrinkles of sorrow sown.
A bundle of fagots bowed her back,
And she was spent with the wrench and rack.
He gave her his loaf and steadied her load
As she took her way on the weary road.
Then to his door came a little child,
Lost and afraid in the world so wild,
In the big, dark world. Catching it up,
He gave it the milk in the waiting cup,
And led it home to its mother's arms,
Out of the reach of the world's alarms.

The day went down in the crimson west
And with it the hope of the blessed Guest,
And Conrad sighed as the world turned gray:
"Why is it, Lord, that your feet delay?
Did You forget that this was the day?"
Then soft in the silence a Voice he heard:
"Lift up your heart, for I kept my word.
Three times I came to your friendly door;
Three times my shadow was on your floor.
I was the beggar with bruised feet;
I was the woman you gave to eat;
I was the child on the homeless street!"

Christmas
Did Not Just Happen

Wilma Fuchs

Christmas was not a happenstance —
    It completed a plan,
Designed eons ago by One
    Who knew the needs of man.

Behind the nativity scene
    A hidden message lies,
Fulfillment of promise to us —
    As well as Three Men Wise.

Back of the trek of the Wise Men,
    Directed by a star,
Man is shown a path to follow
    To heaven's gates ajar.

'Twas in this greatest miracle
    Future hope was avowed,
No, Christmas did not just happen,
    Christmas was made by God.

Painting opposite
THE BIRTH OF CHRIST
by David Ryckaert
Flemish School 1612-1661.

The Tree That Trimmed Itself

Carolyn Sherwin Bailey

The Christmas wind blew through the branches of the young Pine Tree. "I wish, oh, how I wish," it sighed through the wind, "that I might be a Christmas Tree with decorations, just like my brother who was cut down!"

The forest was very still and cold. It was Christmas Eve, the season of wonder. Yet very few trees had been cut for the children. Many tall, strong ones would soon be needed for building homes and for kindling fires and for making furniture. But, oh, the happiness of a Christmas Tree sparkling in the light of the home fire, with a circle of happy children dancing about it! No wonder that the young Pine Tree sighed again through the wind.

"I wish that I might be trimmed for Christmas!" it whispered.

Suddenly something happened there in the forest. Floating down onto the outspread branches of the Pine Tree came white stars, shaped and shining like crystals.

More and still more snow-stars fell, until every twig of every branch of the tree held a white Christmas Star. They were more beautiful than any ornaments that the toyman had for trimming a Christmas Tree.

Still the young Pine Tree longed for all the honors its brother tree would have. "I wish that I might hear the Christmas chimes!" it sighed through the wind.

Then the night grew colder and colder. The frost came through the forest and stopped beside the Pine Tree, hanging sharp, hard icicles to the tips of the twigs. Whenever the wind touched the tree, the icicles tinkled and rang like a chime of tiny bells. They made soft, beautiful Christmas music.

But still the young Pine Tree was not satisfied. "I wish," it sighed, "that I might hold lights as my brother will on this Christmas Eve."

Suddenly the stars shone out in the dark sky and pushed their beams of light down on the branches of the young Pine Tree. One star seemed to leave the sky and rest on the topmost twig of the Pine Tree. There it flamed and flashed like a beacon to call every one to see the wonders of Christmas Eve.

The Pine Tree was lighted as brightly as if it carried a hundred candles, but still it had a wish. "I am not yet a Christmas Tree!" it sighed. "I wish that I might hold gifts among my branches."

It seemed as if this wish could never come true, for where could Christmas gifts be found in the wintry forest?

Christmas Eve changed to the very early dawn of Christmas Day. Still the Pine Tree wore its snow-stars. Its icicle chimes rang in the clear, cold air, and the light of the sky shone in its branches like a Christmas light.

Out from the shelter of a nest among the tree's roots crept the tiny field mice, cold and hungry.

How nice! Hanging to the Pine Tree, just above the nest of the mice, was a bunch of berries and its trailing vine.

The vine had twined itself around the trunk of the Tree in the summer time. Now in the deep winter, its bright berries hung there. They were a gift on Christmas morning for the hungry little mice.

Out from the shelter of the trunk of the Pine Tree came a squirrel. He scampered along one of its branches looking for a cone. But he could not find any. Then he saw a fat brown cone on the ground and hurried down to get it.

The squirrel held the cone daintily in his paws, cut out the seeds and munched them.

They were his holiday breakfast and how good they tasted! No better Christmas gift could have come to the squirrel than those seeds.

Then a gay little snowbird came out from an empty nest among the thick branches of the Pine Tree. It looked around for something to eat. It did not have long to wait.

"Merry Christmas!" called the children, running into the woods later on the morning of Christmas Day. "Merry Christmas, little Pine Tree. We have brought a gift for your snowbird. We heard him calling yesterday."

In their red caps and mittens, the happy children came dancing through the woods with a bundle of ripe wheat. They reached up as far as they could and hung the bundle by a gay red ribbon to one of the branches of the little Pine Tree. Then they exclaimed, and moved back from the tree. For the snowbird soon found the wheat and pecked happily away.

"The snowbird rested in a cradle on Christmas Eve!" the children said to each other. "The little Pine Tree must have held that empty nest very closely all the fall and winter to give the snowbird a Christmas cradle!"

The little Pine Tree stood up straight and happy there on Christmas morning, for all of its wishes had come true. It had trimmed itself with stars and had heard the chimes and had offered its gifts to its little neighbors of the forest. Still it could grow for the building of homes when it was an older, larger pine!

From "The Little Folks' Merry Christmas Book",
used by permission of
Albert Whitman & Co. Publishers.

Painting opposite
NATIVITY
by Clifford Sutherland.

The Story That Never Grows Old

Ottis Shirk

Let us pause and take time again to read
The story so often told,
Of the village obscure, the manger and child —
The story that never grows old.

The shepherds abiding nearby in the field,
Keeping watch o'er their flocks, and then
The Angel's appearance with the Heavenly Host,
Saying, "Peace and good will to men."

The story of the Wise Men from the East
In their journey from afar
In search of Him, born King of the Jews,
Saying, "We have seen His star."

Meditatingly read the old story
In a thoughtful, prayerful way,
And find Bethlehem's child of the manger
Is the hope of the world today.

The Christmas Spirit

Virginia Blanck Moore

When the Christmas spirit springs to life
In the human heart each year,
The world becomes, for a little time,
A haven of love and cheer.

The poor in body are clothed and fed,
And the lonely know once more
The warmth of hearing a welcome knock
On a too long silent door.

For these few days we remember well
That all mankind is kin,
Bound by the love of the Babe who found
No room in that long-ago inn.

But the day goes by, and the spirit dies,
So busy with living are we,
And the poor and the lonely are left once more
In hunger and apathy.

I have been guilty too, God knows,
Too busy to lend a hand,
Too busy to stop for a friendly chat,
Too busy to understand.

"No more, no more let this happen to me,
Dear Lord," I earnestly pray.
"Let me keep the Spirit the whole year through
As bright as it is today."

©

Not Forgotten

Helen Welshimer

I shall place white candles
On every windowsill,
One to face the roadway,
And one to light the hill;

For I have read a story
Which says there was no light
In any house in Bethlehem
That other Christmas night.

Oh, should He come a wanderer,
This night the Christ must see
That when I hung the stockings
And trimmed the Christmas tree,

I turned a shining moment,
From revelry and din,
To place a gracious welcome,
In case He passed my inn.

©

There's Magic

Hilda Butler Farr

There's a magic that comes with Christmas,
A magic that fills the heart,
And it glistens in every window
Of village, in town, or mart.

There's a magic that comes with Christmas,
In Santa and fairy trees,
In the laughter of merry children
And people on bended knees.

There's a magic that comes with Christmas,
A magic for old and young
For it seems that people are kinder
When simple carols are sung.

There's a magic that comes with Christmas
As the scarlet candles glow;
Because Christ was born in a manger
In Bethlehem long ago.

©

ISAIAH

I BRING YOU GOOD TIDINGS OF GREAT JOY

GLORY TO GOD IN THE PEACE GOOD WILL

HIGHEST AND ON EARTH TOWARD MEN LUKE 2:14

Once Upon A Christmastime in the Long Ago

by Erwin L. Hess

Christmastime is that happy season of the year when our thoughts turn to the Christ Child and the most beautiful story ever known. It is a time of the year when the best loved Christmas stories are read and re-read with cherished memories.

Picture opposite
ST. JOHN'S EPISCOPAL CHURCH
Cynwyd, Pennsylvania

The famous old Christmas stories are refreshingly new... and we tell again the pleasant reminiscences of our own Christmas yesterdays.

CHRISTMASTIME IS STORY TIME.
The old favorites add charm to
the joyous Christmas season.
"The Night Before Christmas" was
our childhood's delight......and
Santa appears with his wondrous
reindeer as he streaks off into
the night.
Scrooge defines Christmas and
its true meaning in "A Christmas
Carol" as little Tiny Tim creeps
into our hearts.........
Dearest to us is the old story of
the First Christmas ..the greatest
story... of Mary and Joseph and
the Little Child. The Star that
led the shephards and the Wise-
men to Bethlehem still sheds its
radiant beams.
And the older folks, who live with cherished memories, like to tell of their
own yesterdays, and recall those Christmases of old they love so well....

In the days of long ago...the golden past...there dwelt the real spirit of Christmas...contentment, neighborliness, friendship, gentleness and peace.

Christmas in those days was less hurried and the old-fashioned general store held "very special" gifts for their dear ones. Gifts made at home for each member of the family had love woven and stitched and caressed into them by their own hands. Doll clothes, sleds, woolen mittens and toys for the children..handsome scarves and pretty pin cushions, pot holders and footstools for the grown-ups ...gave such deep meaning when made for each other. What warm memories these things bring!

Back in those yesteryears ....
when Christmas was so simple,
yet so rich...children tried to
be "extra good" when Christmas
drew near. They showed their
holiday delight by doing old-
fashioned chores very willingly.

Keeping the woodbox full
meant cutting and splitting
the logs kept in the shed.
'Twould warm them twice.
Dishes and dusting and
scrubbing, too, were tasks
from which they could not
shirk —'specially near
Christmas.

And then with a glance toward
the North Pole through a Jack
Frosted window..and with a
softly spoken wish, they hoped
that Santa would remember their
angel-like gentleness.

And they like to tell about the old-time happenings which took place just before Christmas . . . . . Grandpa in the workshop as busy as Santa, making secret things of wood and metal . . . . . Father returning from the woods with his ax and a Christmas tree so tall, he could hardly stand it up in the parlor . . . . . Mother in the kitchen . . . . her oven chock full of baking Christmas cookies . . . Oh, can't you smell the spicy aroma!

Pleasant memories indeed... and folks like to recall how Grandpa climbed the ladder to the roof on Christmas Eve and traced sly "tracks" in the snow, and large boot "prints". How many years passed by before they learned of Grandpa's traditional ladder climb? Those old-time Christmases were so nice....

Town folks and country folks alike were knitted together in true neighborliness, 'specially on Christmas Eve ...when the snow was soft and sparkling in the light of the lamps and the lanterns. The silence was broken only by the chiming of the bells in the steeples ... and by the bells jingling on the sleighs, as friends and neighbors celebrated the Infant's birthday in the gentle way. Churches shone brightly as their doors opened for Christmas services.

In the front parlors, families from near and far gathered around the festive trees which gleamed with lighted candles. The soft dazzle and shimmer of one of those great fir trees in the quaint old room is still before the eyes of those who remember.... long strings of silver tinsel draped in gentle festoons from its branches from crest to base ... a thousand shiny ornaments hung from its branch tips ... candy canes ... candy cherries on thin wires ... and cornucopias stuffed with special sweets. What wonderful memories.

The grownups would tell the old stories of Santa Claus in the old-fashioned way, remembering how in days past he brought their first pair of ice skates that they just HAD to try out on the old grist mill pond ... even though the temperature had dropped to eight degrees below! In the morning there was the thrill and excitement of seeing Santa's presents spread below the big tree... the popping of ribbon and string...the tearing and shredding of paper..the opening of boxes...the shrieks of laughter and delight...true ecstacy as childhood's cup overflowed. And, the happy smiles of the old folks as they opened up their own presents. Being remembered in such a loving way by friends and family, their spectacles steamed up ... that only a dab of a 'kerchief could remedy.

Folks like to remember and tell how they used to rejoice with a grateful prayer at midnight and in the morning, too, just like we do today. Only those were more tranquil days. Yes, Christmastime is story time... remembering time. The Holy Story of the little Babe in Bethlehem is told again... and we reflect the true meaning of Christmas with its warm, nostalgic feeling... and we long for those dear, dear days of yesteryear.

Because Once, Long Ago

Reba Mahan Stevens

Still Bethlehem the town
Lies where it lay long years ago,
Its olive orchards basking in the sun,
Its hillsides set with lilies red and white.

Still brown-faced children play
Through crooked streets
And wander on the hills;
Still men sow seed and harvest grain;
Still women bake;
Still runs life's endless circle
Round and round,
And common days are filled with common toil.

But all the world
Goes the more bravely to its task
Because once, long ago,
A Little Child was born
In Bethlehem.

©

Twelfth Night

Nancy Byrd Turner

There were three dim shadows speaking low
In the hollow behind the hill.
(Bethlehem's homes, a crooked row,
Were dumb in the dark, and still.)
One was a stranger, late come in,
Four tired beasts to stall,
One was Joel, the stable boy,
And the third was Enos, a shepherd lad,
And a star shone over them all.

The stranger speaks:

He said, "We have traveled for many a day,
I know not whither or why,
The sun beat down on an endless way —
The desert, bare as the sky,
On and on, while the hot sand swirled
'Neath the camels' cleaving feet,
Till the sun dropped over the rim of the world
And blessed dark fell sweet.
Their talk was all of a single star,
Their eyes were fain for its light.
A wondrous thing, when we stopped to sleep
It made a flame in the night.
And when I wakened to stir the beasts,
Daily as dawn blew chill,
My masters asked, 'Is it shining now?
And I said, it is shining still."

The shepherd lad speaks:

He said, "I was far on the hills that night,
For a lamb had come to harm.
I was bringing it back by the lower brook
Fast asleep on my arm,
When sudden a light in the sky, a light,
A glory above the fold —
Not like the moonrise — radiant, white,
Ah, it can never be told!
The cry of the shepherds came to me,
I caught it sharp from the hill,
And music answering, wild and free —
Surely I hear it still!
Then a hush, and dark, and the men came down,
I marked the way they went,
Silent and eager toward the town,
But I knew not what it meant."

The stable boy speaks:

He said, "I had toiled in the dust all day
At the people's beck and call,
When two worn travelers came to pray
For room in an empty stall.
I gave them place, and I flung me late
In the straw by the well to sleep.
I heard the guard move down by the gate,
And the cattle breathing deep.
Then, far in the night, the oxen stirred;
I roused and listened a space.
A tremor, a sigh, a whispered word,
A finger of light on my face —
Light? . . . . . To the stable door I crept,
And lo, a circle of flame
Hovered fair at the manger's head,
But I knew not whence it came."

Closer they drew, the wondering three,
In the hollow behind the hill.
They said, "By many a mystery
The great God works His will."

And they fell on their knees for love and awe
In the dark of Bethlehem's wall —
The swarthy stranger who rode from far,
The stable boy and the shepherd lad —
And the Star shone over them all.

©

His Coming

Della Adams Leitner

He might have come from heaven
In splendor, crowned with light —
Spectacular and regal,
An awe-inspiring sight.

He might have come triumphant,
A leader or a king
With armies and with banners
'Mid throngs that homage bring.

He might have come a mystic,
Philosopher or sage,
Acknowledged as the greatest
By wise men of His age.

But God who is our Father,
With His great Father-heart,
Sent Jesus as a baby
That He might thus impart
His perfect loving message
Heard that first Christmas morn,
It holds all hope, all promise,
"To you a Child is born."

©

Only The Young

Daniel Whitehead Hicky

Only the young will brave the snow
And catch the flakes and watch them go
In swirling patterns up and down
The length and breadth of all the town.

Only the young can laugh to see
White, sudden blossoms on a tree
That were not there an hour ago,
Or lift their hearts to see the snow
Reach out its hand and turn the night
Into a wonderland of white.

The old will rise and turn the lock
When frozen fists of snowflakes knock
Upon the pane, along the sill,
And break the pine trees on the hill.
The old will draw the curtains tight
And have no traffic with the night.

But they will stir the fire and pile
The hearth with logs, and afterwhile,
When they are nodding in its glow,
Live once again lost years of snow.

He Who Walks Through Snow

Harry Elmore Hurd

He who walks through snow may see
The transformation of a tree . . .

A pine, as lofty as a tower,
Suddenly becomes a flower —

The whiteness of a hemlock's lace
Makes fairyland of any place.

Blossoms tuft the clustered seeds
Of the inflorescent weeds.

The crimson fire of sumac flame
Gives to loveliness a name.

No word is said — there is no sound
Of petals falling to the ground —

But O, the things a man may know
Who walks alone through silent snow!

Picture opposite
SNOW CLAD PINE BOUGHS
High Sierras, California

A Child Again

William A. Washburn

Most of all the time I like to think
That all my childish ways
Are but mementos of the past:
Forgotten yesterdays;
But once a year, at Christmastime,
There comes a sudden change,
The years don't seem to count for much —
I'm just a child again.

The decorated Christmas tree
Adorned with angel's hair;
A dad and mother, hearts made light,
With all their children there;
Some simple gifts that speak of love,
Each a surprise to bring,
When all these things come to my mind —
I'm just a child again.

We've all been taught that Christmastime
Is just for girls and boys —
The little tots who like to play
With dolls, and blocks, and toys —
Perhaps it is, but when gay hearts
The Christmas carols sing,
The years don't mean a thing to me —
I'm just a child again.

©

Picture opposite
GRAND TETON PEAKS
Jackson Hole, Wyoming

No Calendar Needed

Lolita Pinney

For many years a calendar
  hung on our kitchen wall
And Mother checked the busy days
  and seasons as they'd fall,
But no calendar was needed
  to know the time of year:
By the fragrance of her kitchen,
  I knew the season near!

The aroma of hot chile
  when the wintry air was cold;
The rhubarb custards cooling
  when spring's magic would unfold;
Bubbling jellies in the kettle
  when the summer heat was high;
And in frosty, tangy autumn,
  whiffs of spicy pumpkin pie!

True, no calendar was needed
  for an eager child to know
That Christmas time was coming!
  Mother hurried to and fro

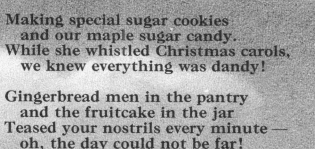

Making special sugar cookies
  and our maple sugar candy.
While she whistled Christmas carols,
  we knew everything was dandy!

Gingerbread men in the pantry
  and the fruitcake in the jar
Teased your nostrils every minute —
  oh, the day could not be far!
We cracked nutmeats on the flatiron,
  and strung popcorn for the tree
And every hour was heaven
  in the kitchen, seems to me!

Mother in her big white apron
  with some flour on her cheek
Is the dearest recollection
  of my cherished Christmas week;
A calendar was useless,
  but the essence was bewitchin'
And you always knew 'twas Christmas
  by the fragrance in the kitchen!

©

In Lowly Places

Mrs. Roy L. Peifer

Sometimes in the lowliest places
The most wondrous of treasures are found,
The most brilliant and precious diamonds
Buried deep in the blackest ground.

'Twas a strange place to seek for a King —
In a stable, lowly and bare —
But shepherds from Judean hills
Found the little Lord Jesus there.

©

Picture opposite
MOUNT SUPERIOR
Wasatch Mountains, Utah

On A Frosty Winter Night

La Verne P. Larson

Have you ever felt the magic
On a frosty winter night,
When you walked within a wonderland
Of crystal flakes of white?

It brings back joyful memories
Of the days of long ago,
When your heart found perfect happiness
In gentle falling snow.

You remember many happy times,
The snow forts that you built,
Each chubby smiling snowman
With his funny hat atilt.

The sleigh rides and the laughter
All seem to echo still,
And again you see your merry friends
Who slid upon the hill.

A snowfall's magic wonder
Brings back the long ago,
And if you don't believe me
Take an evening walk in snow.

©

Picture opposite
BIRCH ON SNOWY LANE
New Hampshire

Snow Storm

Ethel Romig Fuller

All day the old earth waited;
The clouds hung gray and low;
Then in the brief and sudden dusk
It began to snow —

Flake by soft, white, feathery flake,
Until the rusty, brown
Hedgerows and the apple trees
Were swathed in eiderdown.

And all the bare fields round about,
And every rounded hill —
It snowed that night, it snowed next day,
It snowed and snowed until
Away across the countryside,
As far as eye could see,
Were no familiar landmarks, where
A fence or bush should be.

©

Snowy Roads

Grace A. Buttrick

O little snowy roads of Christmas, winding
Toward homes with laurelled doors and window-light,
To warmth and cheer and Yuletide fire, finding
The Christ Child seeking birth with men, tonight.

O little snowy roads of Christmas, leading
To homes, sweet scent of fir and candlelight,
To yielding hearts the mystery conceding,
The Christ Child seeking birth with men, tonight.

©

Picture opposite
WINTER WONDERLAND
Arizona

The Buying of Gifts

Grace Noll Crowell

When I was a child on my father's farm,
And Christmastime drew near,
I would trudge thru the snow to the little town . . .
Oh, the memory is quite clear
Of the little girl with a quarter to spend
For parents, for brother, and sister, and friend.

My scarlet mittens and scarlet hood
Were white with glistening snow,
My eyes were shining with eagerness,
My frost-bright cheeks aglow,
As I went gladly, hurrying down
To the novelty store in the little town.

And oh, the rapture, the sheer delight!
The shop's small windows shone
With beautiful things . . . and there was I
With a quarter all my own!
I searched — and will wonders never cease?
I found five gifts for a nickel apiece.

Such beautiful gifts! And trudging home
Thru the winter dusk, I knew
A joy and a glowing happiness
That has lasted the long years thru.
For something of that far Christmastime
Stayed in my heart and it still is mine.

Only A Little Town

Esther Baldwin York

On all the other nights it had been only a little town, half-hidden in the darkness.

Then came that Night of Nights when Light came to Bethlehem. There was the dazzling glory of the angel choir brightening the skies of the surrounding country. There was the pure white light of the Star that stood over a stable roof. There was the golden radiance emanating from the Baby in the manger, making beautiful the humble stable and everything in it. There was the light of happiness in Mary's eyes and the light of love and wonder in the eyes of all who came to behold the little Saviour.

Light travels fast and far. And the Light from Bethlehem still shines brightly today in the hearts of all who love Him.

Time Long Ago

Ora Pate Stewart

Time long ago, on an Indian Summer night,
When the harvest was put away,
And children were snuggled in feather beds
At close of a busy day —

Then Father would sit at the open hearth
And fashion with knife and scroll
A hobby horse, or a sturdy sled,
Or maybe a wooden doll —
While Mother maneuvered the crochet hook,
Or schemed with the calico . . .
And fascinators and pinafores
Danced polkas in a row.

It isn't that world economy
Has untethered his silver wings . . .
But that, atticked away in a cob-webbed age,
Lies the pleasure of making things.

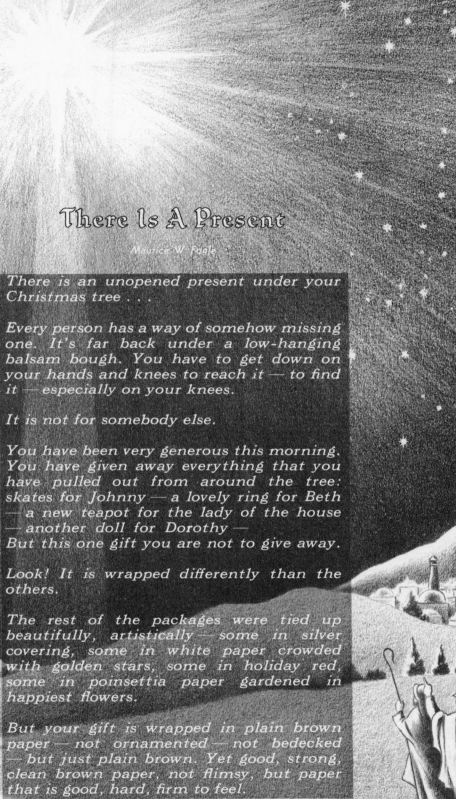

There Is A Present

Maurice W. Fogle

There is an unopened present under your
Christmas tree . . .

Every person has a way of somehow missing
one. It's far back under a low-hanging
balsam bough. You have to get down on
your hands and knees to reach it — to find
it — especially on your knees.

It is not for somebody else.

You have been very generous this morning.
You have given away everything that you
have pulled out from around the tree:
skates for Johnny — a lovely ring for Beth
— a new teapot for the lady of the house
— another doll for Dorothy —
But this one gift you are not to give away.

Look! It is wrapped differently than the
others.

The rest of the packages were tied up
beautifully, artistically — some in silver
covering, some in white paper crowded
with golden stars, some in holiday red,
some in poinsettia paper gardened in
happiest flowers.

But your gift is wrapped in plain brown
paper — not ornamented — not bedecked
— but just plain brown. Yet good, strong,
clean brown paper, not flimsy, but paper
that is good, hard, firm to feel.

Well-tied, too, this bundle . . . No, not in that labyrinth of knots which make of a package a prison and require the slash of liberating scissors, but just well tied.

Now you are almost ready to open it!

Then you remember you ought to look and see where the gift is from and who sent it, or placed it mysteriously beneath the tree.

It is then you discover that while the paper of the package is very plain, there is nothing plain about the sending address, or the signature of the sender up in the left-hand corner.

With what kind of ink was this written? It must have been mingled with star-shine, for it glitters and glistens and gleams.

It is hardly like ink at all, but is a kind of fluid with which all letters of remembrance ought to be written, all love told, all greetings engraved.

Should not all people, noticing the place where the gift came from, touch it with lingering fingers, and handle it in chastened manner?

An address!
You have never had a present from this place before? Think hard about that, my friend.

Yes, you did!

Do you remember when life was too cold and distant to hand out presents, and you were too far away to be reached by those who loved you and wanted to reach you, but you were too far away, too lonely, too elusive?

Yet there was the giving and the gift which came in that shining, surprising hour. So you were softly lifted, and sustained.

You never received a gift from this Person before?

Or, do you pause with a strange hesitancy at the awesome dignity of that name?

Only three letters there, yet those letters, by some artistic perspective stand so high — as high indeed as redwood trees or un-mastered peaks.

And the three letters reach so wide as if to include all the alphabets that have ever been printed and spell all that they have spelt.

This is the name that is unforgettable — the name of the Sender . . .

Imprinted as deeply as the stars upon the heavens, registered in every history of time, but marked in the corner of your Christmas gift special to you . . . and winged by fastest delivery and quickest kindness in Love's stratospheric plane on Christmas Eve.

Start opening the package then, but as the wrappings fall away — stop! For there is that lovely instant of anticipation, that glad, precious moment when you don't quite know — yet you almost know.

Then, there it is — the Gift!

The gift is FAITH . . .

Not a flimsy, fluttering Faith that dissolves with the slightest blow, for there is granite-greatness in it, and mountain-firmness and power, and it is in sufficient amount to last from one year to the next — for every day in-between one Christmas and another.

This Faith is practical.

You who are wife and mother, as Mary was, will find that it helps in crowded corners, and in tightened-up emergency hours when your own are dreadfully in danger.

This Faith will keep you unshaken when storms assail — it will work miracles which you, being close to birth, and life, and love, will see . . . And you will believe, as she believed, in her heart's bravery.

You, who like Joseph, labor in a shop will find this Faith good. There will be days when the wheels won't spin and levers will jam, but somehow the good workman's patience and ingenuity will prevail. And you will say, "I can, for FAITH can!"

Sometimes, of course, Faith will have more than everyday reliable plainness. It will have the Bethlehem quality — the glory of the meadows of heaven and the celestial rapture of the heavenly host.

On Christmas morn it is yours, this gift.

Over it, the Great Giver smiled, even Himself as He somehow got it tucked into a plain, brown package, pushed too far back to see, under the Christmas tree.

Painting opposite
MADONNA AND CHILD
by Joseph Maniscalco

As Fine A Friend As You

Albert Kennedy Rowswell

At Christmas time when joy bells ring
And hearts are light and gay,
We turn the pages back again
For just one fleeting day.

And there the friends of yesteryear
Pass by in swift review —
It's something to have lived and known
As fine a friend as you.

Sometimes the skies have been o'ercast
The sun refused to shine;
Sometimes the road has weary been
And hope was on decline;

But always came the cheering thought
And courage would renew —
It's something to have lived and known
As fine a friend as you.

At Christmas time when hearts rejoice
And all the world seems fair —
When selfishness is put aside,
We've happiness to share;

May fortune smile on you and yours
And light your path anew —
It's something to have lived and known
As fine a friend as you.

Behold,
a virgin shall conceive, and bear a son, and shall call his name

Immanuel.

Isaiah 7:14

It Is Christmas Once More

Loretta Bauer Buckley

It is Christmas once more. Do you remember, when your world was very young, how you jumped into bed and counted on your fingers just how many days it would be until that glorious day arrived? Lying snug and warm in your featherbed you saw a thousand glittering angel-topped trees in the dark; heard the prancing of Dasher and Dancer on the attic roof. Even the branches of the old maple, storm-tossed against your window, played a Yuletide melody.

There was so much to be done in the last few hours before Santa's visit that you scarcely took time to breathe. In the flurry of excitement mother developed the art of moving in all directions at once and you had to be constantly shooed from underfoot.

The fragrance that came from the kitchen skyrocketed your anticipation of good things to come — mace, cinnamon, nutmeg. Not to mention ginger cookies and fresh bread cooling on the sturdy table. The pantry bulged with vegetables, apples and jars of golden fruit brought up from the cellar. Do you remember making sure there were spiced peaches because you liked those best?

Bringing in wood for the fireplace in the "company" parlor became a pleasure. And shoveling a path through the snow from the porch all the way to the woodshed was a chore you really wanted to do. The spirit of giving and doing filled every inch of your small frame.

And what fun it was going into the woods to chop down the Christmas tree! Though the icy wind stiffened your nose and ears, the glow in your

heart more than made up for the pain you knew. As the tree was placed in the barn, you were certain you heard a baby's cry come from the hayloft. You had prepared a crib — and did not miracles happen at Christmastide? Frankincense and myrrh were strange-sounding gifts, so you left part of a nameless joy you felt there beside the small manger. . .

Once in the parlor the redolence of the tall fir, as the warmth of the room touched it, cast a perfume you said you would never forget. And you promised to remember always the ruby red cranberry chains that swung gayly from its emerald branches.

The ritual of hanging your stocking was one that shattered your heart into diamond-like fragments of happiness. You could never find a word for that enchanted moment — even to this day. Then to bed, and 'though the floor was as cold as the pond on which you hoped to try your new skates, you did not leave out a single prayer. The first one was for the Baby Jesus, and the last for the safety of Saint Nicholas.

The eve of Christmas is upon us once again. Candles of memory flame brightly over the years and the miles of drifted snow. In your dreams tonight may you hear the cry of the New Born King as you heard it in childhood's golden hours; songs of herald angels; shepherds' sandaled steps on Bethlehem's starlit road. And may you wake to a world grown miraculously new, beautiful beyond belief, because a Little Child came into it with the gift of perfect love for all men.

Holy Night

And there were in the same country shepherds abiding in the field, keeping watch over their flock by night.

And, lo, the angel of the Lord came upon them, and the glory of the Lord shone round about them: and they were sore afraid.

And the angel said unto them, Fear not: for, behold I bring you good tidings of great joy, which shall be to all people.

For unto you is born this day in the city of David a Saviour, which is Christ the Lord.

And this shall be a sign unto you: Ye shall find the babe wrapped in swaddling clothes, lying in a manger.

And suddenly there was with the angel a multitude of the heavenly host praising God, and saying,

Glory to God in the highest, and on earth peace, good will toward men.

Luke 2: 8-14

ENGROSSED BY KATE KRAUSE BALL, IN THE YEAR OF OUR LORD, 1949, AND FOR HIS GLORY

The Star In The East

Clara Moote

The star in the east is shining again
For the eyes of the world to see
It stops once more o'er Bethlehem
Where the manger used to be.

It shines on the spot where the crowded inn
Had no room for Mother with Child —

It shines on the fields where shepherds were
Minding their flocks so mild.

It shines on the road the wise men took
As they followed its rays so bright
And knelt at the feet of the new born Child
That brought to the world God's Light.

Oh, lift your eyes to the eastern star
That shines in the heavens tonight,
And feel the glory the wise men felt
And be bathed in its wondrous light.

The Story of the

Wise Men

Now when Jesus was born in Bethlehem of Judaea in the days of Herod the king, behold, there came wise men from the east to Jerusalem,

Saying, Where is he that is born King of the Jews? for we have seen his star in the east, and are come to worship him. — — — —

When Herod the king had heard these things, he was troubled, and all Jerusalem with him. — — — — —

And when he had gathered all the chief priests and scribes of the people together, he demanded of them where Christ should be born. —

And they said unto him, In Bethlehem of Judaea: for thus it is written by the prophet, — — — — — — —

And thou Bethlehem, in the land of Juda, art not the least among the princes of Juda: for out of thee shall come a Governor, that shall rule my people of Israel. — — — — — —

Then Herod, when he had privily called the wise men, enquired of them diligently what time the star appeared. — — — —

And he sent them to Bethlehem, and said, Go and search diligently for the young child; and when ye have found him, bring me word again, that I may come and worship him also. — — — —

When they had heard the king, they departed; and, lo, the star, which they saw in the east, went before them, till it came and stood over where the young child was. — — — — —

When they saw the star, they rejoiced with exceeding great joy.

And when they were come into the house, they saw the young child with Mary his mother, and fell down, and worshipped him: and when they had opened their treasures, they presented him gifts; gold, and frankincense, and myrrh. — — — — —

And being warned of God in a dream that they should not return to Herod, they departed into their own country another way. — —

Matthew 2: 1–12

ENGROSSED BY KATE KRAUSH BALL IN THE YEAR OF OUR LORD · 1950 · AND FOR HIS GLORY

O Christmas Tree

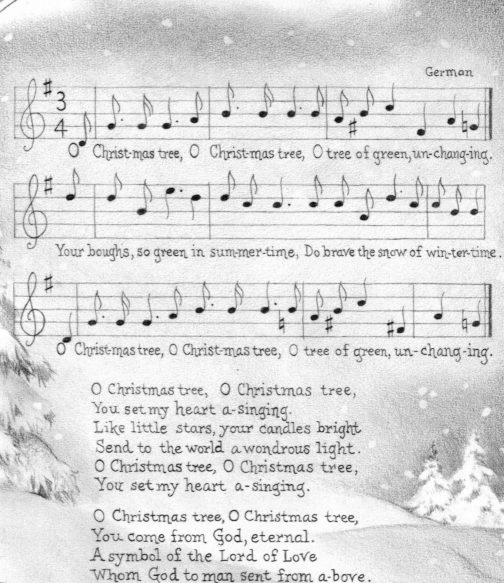

German

O Christ-mas tree, O Christ-mas tree, O tree of green, un-chang-ing.

Your boughs, so green in sum-mer-time, Do brave the snow of win-ter-time.

O Christ-mas tree, O Christ-mas tree, O tree of green, un-chang-ing.

O Christmas tree, O Christmas tree,
You set my heart a-singing.
Like little stars, your candles bright
Send to the world a wondrous light.
O Christmas tree, O Christmas tree,
You set my heart a-singing.

O Christmas tree, O Christmas tree,
You come from God, eternal.
A symbol of the Lord of Love
Whom God to man sent from a-bove.
O Christmas tree, O Christmas tree,
You come from God, eternal.

O Christmas tree, O Christmas tree,
You speak of God, unchanging.
You tell us all to faithful be,
And trust in God eternally.
O Christmas tree, O Christmas tree,
You speak of God eternally.

JINGLE BELL

Vera Hardman

A little elf helped Santa Claus
His name was Jingle Bell,
I guess there wasn't anything
He couldn't do quite well.

He painted the wooden soldiers
And dressed the dollies' hair,
He saw the bounce was right in balls
And was 'most everywhere.

He even dipped the chocolates
And striped the candy canes,
He always trimmed the little trees
That grew in Christmas Lane.

When Christmas Eve was here at last
He packed old Santa's sleigh —
And checked on all of the reindeer
'Ere he was on his way.

Now Santa Claus had never asked
Jingle Bell to come along,
He felt that he deserved his rest
For working all year long.

But Jingle Bell felt differently,
He wished to ride the sleigh,
He wanted to help Santa Claus
And climb the Milky Way.

This Christmas Eve old Santa Claus
Saw Jingle Bell was sad
Suddenly he knew the reason
And how to make him glad.

So he tucked him in beside him
And he was truly gay,
As they sang the songs of Christmas
As they journeyed on their way.

It was joy to fill the stockings
And trim the Christmas tree,
A gayer, little elf I'm sure
Could never, never be.

So if on Christmas Day you find
Your stocking stuffed quite well,
You'll know that Santa's helper
Was little Jingle Bell.

A Santa Claus Cookie

Anne Campbell

A small thing to cherish,
  a trifle to prize,
This Santa Claus cookie
  with raisins for eyes!

He came home and carried it
  proudly to me.
"I got it," he said, "from
  the Sunday School tree!"

A fat man, a round man
  who's chubby and wise,
A Santa Claus cookie
  with raisins for eyes.

He may not remember,
  this dearest of boys,
The books Santa brought him,
  the games and the toys.

When he is a man all these pleasures will dim,
  The train that he cherished, the drum given him.
But back in his mind he will keep this surprise:
  A Santa Claus cookie with raisins for eyes.

The Life of Santa Claus

Florence Granquist Ray

Deep in the country of snows up and down,
Far in the northland — away from a town,
Santa's old house of remarkable charm,
Lies in the snowdrifts that cover his farm.

All of the windows you see in the night,
Are bordered with snow and shining with light.
All through the evenings, and all through the year,
The light you can see, and the noise you can hear.

Painting opposite
ARCTIC SLED DOG
by Jack Greiner

Busy old Santa, so happy and wise,
Is making new toys for a Christmas surprise..
Sawing and pounding and painting away,
Colorful things for the next Christmas Day.

Out of the chimney, the smoke rises high,
Straight through the air to the stars in the sky;
Up from the fireplace crackling and warm,
Out in the cold . . . and the wind . . . and the storm.

Dear Mrs. Santa is busy within,
Reading to Santa the letters for him;
Cooking and sewing and lending a hand,
Dressing new dolls for the girls of the land;

Knitting their sweaters and curling their hair,
Tying their bonnets and slippers to wear;
Rocking them softly to sleep with a song,
Thoughtfully sending their blankets along.

Just a short way from the big kitchen door,
Stands the old barn with a rough wooden floor . . .
Snuggled against a white hillside of snow,
Cozy and warm for the reindeer, you know.

Day after day, every morning and night,
Santa goes out with a lantern for light,
Pumping the water for all of the deer,
Feeding them hay from the loft that is near.

Patting them gently . . . each one in his stall,
Jingling the sleighbells that hang on the wall,
Calling their names; for they listen, and know
Santa will take them out in the snow.

Back to the barn go the reindeer once more.
Santa has finished his everyday chore;
Up to the house and right on with his work,
(Never a moment would Santa Claus shirk.)

All through the day, and far into the night,
Year after year and with all of his might,
Santa is busy — as busy can be
Making good presents for you and for me.

Deep in the country of snows up and down,
Far in the Northland — is Santa Claus town.

©

Jolly Old Saint Nicholas

When the clock is strik-ing twelve, when I'm fast a-sleep,

Down the chimney broad and black, With your pack you'll creep;

All the stock-ings you will find Hang-ing in a row;

Mine will be the short-est one; You'll be sure to know.

The Night Before Christmas

Clement Clarke Moore

'Twas the night before Christmas, when all through the house
Not a creature was stirring, not even a mouse;
The stockings were hung by the chimney with care,
In hopes that St. Nicholas soon would be there;

The children were nestled all snug in their beds,
While visions of sugar-plums danced in their heads;
And Mamma in her kerchief, and I in my cap,
Had just settled our brains for a long winter's nap,

When out on the lawn there arose such a clatter,
I sprang from my bed to see what was the matter.
Away to the window I flew like a flash,
Tore open the shutters and threw up the sash.

The moon, on the breast of the new-fallen snow,
Gave a luster of mid-day to objects below;
When, what to my wandering eyes should appear,
But a miniature sleigh, and eight tiny reindeer,
With a little old driver, so lively and quick,
I knew in a moment it must be St. Nick.

More rapid than eagles his coursers they came,
And he whistled, and shouted, and called them by name:
"Now, Dasher! now, Dancer! now, Prancer and Vixen!
On, Comet! on, Cupid! on, Donder and Blitzen!
To the top of the porch, to the top of the wall!
Now, dash away, dash away, dash away, all!"

As dry leaves that before the wild hurricane fly,
When they meet with an obstacle, mount to the sky,
So, up to the house-top the coursers they flew,
With a sleigh full of toys — and St. Nicholas, too.

And then in a twinkling I heard on the roof
The prancing and pawing of each little hoof.
As I drew in my head, and was turning around,
Down the chimney St. Nicholas came with a bound.

He was dressed all in fur from his head to his foot,
And his clothes were all tarnished with ashes and soot;
His droll little mouth was drawn up like a bow,
And the beard on his chin was as white as the snow.

The stump of a pipe he held tight in his teeth,
And the smoke it encircled his head like a wreath;
A bundle of toys he had flung on his back,
And he looked like a peddler just opening his pack.

His eyes how they twinkled! his dimples how merry!
His cheeks were like roses, his nose like a cherry;
He had a broad face and a little round belly
That shook when he laughed, like a bowlful of jelly.

He was chubby and plump — a right jolly old elf;
And I laughed when I saw him, in spite of myself.
A wink of his eye, and a twist of his head,
Soon gave me to know I had nothing to dread.

He spoke not a word, but went straight to his work,
And filled all the stockings; then turned with a jerk
And laying his finger aside of his nose,
And giving a nod, up the chimney he rose.

He sprang to his sleigh, to his team gave a whistle,
And away they all flew like the down of a thistle;
But I heard him exclaim ere he drove out of sight,
"Happy Christmas to all, and to all a goodnight!"

COMET

CUPID

DONDER

BLITZEN

CANDY CANES

Kathryn Jackson

Candy canes have the nicest way
Of lasting long after Christmas Day.
For, after you've eaten two from down low,
And maybe one from up high —
You just can't manage to eat some more
No matter how hard you try.

But after the Christmas tree is gone,
And the cookies and candy, too —
And it's January, and dark and gray,
And there's nothing much to do,
And you wish for something to nibble on
While it sleets and freezes and rains,
Why, up on the shelf in a big glass jar,
There are always some candy canes.

They're mostly always
broken in bits,
And sticky, and
stuck with pine,
And hard to unstick,
and hard to get out —
But they taste
most specially fine,

All broken the size to fit your mouth,
All syrupy, peppermint sweet,
All Christmasy red and white, and then —
Why, there's nothing so good to eat
As candy canes, with their very nice way
Of lasting long after Christmas Day.

From the Big Golden Book THE SANTA CLAUS BOOK, written
and compiled by Kathryn Jackson; copyright 1952 by
Simon and Schuster, Inc., and Artists and Writers Guild, Inc.
Reprinted by permission.

The Lovely Days of Winter

Kalfus Kurtz

The lovely days of winter come,
The wind is like a muffled drum.

I did not miss this pastel sky
When summer roses bloomed nearby;

I did not know that on this hill
There was such beauty, chaste and still;

That mirrored ice in frozen stream
Could catch and hold a vagrant dream;

That tall bare trees so hard and brown
Could sing though leaves had fluttered down —

But now with new-found joy I see
All that the summer hid from me.

Painting opposite
CHRISTMAS WONDERLAND
by Miki

Reprinted from THIS WEEK Magazine. Copyright 1939
by the United Newspapers Magazine Corporation.
Our sincere thanks to the author whose address we were
unable to locate.

What Christmas Is As We Grow Older

Charles Dickens
(1812 — 1870)

Time was, with most of us, when Christmas Day, encircling all our limited world like a magic ring, left nothing out for us to miss or seek; bound together all our home enjoyments, affections, and hopes; grouped everything and every one around the Christmas fire; and made the little picture shining in our bright young eyes complete.

And is our life here, at the best, so constituted that, pausing as we advance at such a noticeable milestone in the track as this great birthday, we look back on the things that never were, as naturally and full as gravely as on the things that have been and are gone, or have been and still are? If it be so, and so it seems to be, must we come to the conclusion that life is little better than a dream, and little worth the loves and strivings that we crowd into it?

No! Far be such miscalled philosophy from us, dear reader, on Christmas Day! Nearer and closer to our hearts be the Christmas spirit, which is the spirit of active usefulness, perseverance, cheerful discharge of duty, kindness, and forbearance! It is in the last virtues especially that we are, or should be, strengthened by the unaccomplished visions of our youth; for, who shall say that they are not our teachers, to deal gently even with the impalpable nothings of the earth!

Welcome, old aspirations, glittering creatures of an ardent fancy, to your shelter underneath the holly! We know you, and have not outlived you yet. Welcome, old projects and old loves, however fleeting, to your nooks among the steadier lights that burn around us. Welcome, all that was ever real to our hearts; and for the earnestness that made you real, thanks to heaven!

Welcome everything! Welcome alike what has been, and what never was, and what we hope may be, to your shelter underneath the holly, to your places round the Christmas fire, where what is, sits open-hearted!

Of all days in the year, we will turn our faces toward that City upon Christmas Day, and from its silent hosts bring those we loved among us. In the Blessed Name wherein we are gathered together at this time, and in the Presence that is here among us according to the promise, we will receive, and not dismiss, the people who were dear to us!

The winter sun goes down over town and village; on the sea it makes a rosy path, as if the Sacred Tread were fresh upon the water. A few more moments, and it sinks, and night comes on, and lights begin to sparkle in the prospect. In town and village, there are doors and windows closed against the weather; there are flaming logs heaped high; there are joyful faces; there is healthy music of voices. Be all ungentleness and harm excluded from the temples of the household gods, but be those memories admitted with tender encouragement! They are of Time and all its comforting and peaceful reassurances; and of the broad beneficence and goodness that too many men have tried to tear to narrow shreds.

Legacy

Rachel Van Creme

A new year is a magic chest,
Untold wealth is in it;
A golden chain of precious hours —
Every link a minute.

Tears and laughter, sadness, song —
Jeweled gems that lend
Richness to the legacy . . .
Ours to keep or spend.

A new year is a magic chest;
The gift of time is in it.
So guard it well, and do not lose
One precious, golden minute!

©

ideals

PUBLISHING CO.
3510 W. ST. PAUL AVE.
MILWAUKEE 1, WIS.

from the desk of
VAN B. HOOPER
editor

Dear Friend of IDEALS,

Now that you have finished reading CHRISTMAS IDEALS -

May I add just a short personal note?

I hope sincerely that you have enjoyed thoroughly each page of
this Christmas issue -

That it has brought to you the richness and deep meaning of this
special season.

May I suggest that you share this Christmas warmth and
inspiration with others by sending them an IDEALS gift copy or
an IDEALS gift subscription -

Can you appreciate the happiness and joy your gift copy of
CHRISTMAS IDEALS - for only $1.50 each - will bring to the
hearts of your friends and relatives?

A gift subscription, too, for a full year of IDEALS - at $5.00 -
will keep your Christmas remembrance gift fresh and new all
year 'round.

From the comfort of your armchair - just send us a list of the
folks you want to remember in this special way.

Fill out the attached order form and mail it to us with your
remittance. The folks at IDEALS will be proud to handle your
order carefully and promptly.

Your OWN copies of CHRISTMAS IDEALS that you direct to be
sent to you will be placed in the mail as soon as possible after
we receive your order.

All of your GIFT CHRISTMAS IDEALS will be placed in the mail,
postpaid, about December 10th - to arrive at just the right time
during the Christmas Season.

I urge you to send your orders to us TODAY. We shall be
delighted to hear from you.

And now -

I would like to extend my deep and sincere wishes for a
healthful, happy Christmas-time to you - and to those good
friends that you want to remember this year with IDEALS gifts.

Cordially,

Van B. Hooper

editor

Christmas
ISSUE
ideals

As the name implies — IDEALS are exquisite issues of clean, wholesome, old-fashioned ideals — homey philosophy — poetry — art — music — inspiration — neighborliness — things many of us may have overlooked during these busy days.

IDEALS are published QUARTERLY — about every ninety days — one for each season of the year.

Your own subscription to a series of beautiful issues of IDEALS will be a cherished, precious addition to your personal library.

A GIFT SUBSCRIPTION to this consecutive series of IDEALS for FAMILY — FRIENDS — RELATIVES — NEIGHBORS — PASTOR — TEACHER and BUSINESS ASSOCIATES — makes a perfect, long-remembered gift.

A lovely Gift announcement will be sent to the recipient of your GIFT SUBSCRIPTION to herald your thoughtfulness with a ONE YEAR SUBSCRIPTION to a series of IDEALS.

SINGLE ISSUES OF IDEALS

only $1.50 per copy

Ideals Subscription Plans

★

ONE YEAR   4 issues as published   *only* $5.00

TWO YEARS   8 issues as published   *only* $10.00

★

PAY-AS-YOU-READ 1 copy each issue as published — about every ninety days. A reserved copy will be sent AUTOMATICALLY with an invoice for $1.50. $1.50 per copy

★

IDEALS scheduled to follow CHRISTMAS IDEALS —

EASTER IDEALS (March 15, 1958)
A reverent and joyous portrayal of the Easter Season told in poetry, art reproductions, and select articles. This issue depicts, artistically, the Easter spirit and the magnificence of Spring.

ADVENTURE IDEALS (June 1, 1958)
A colorful issue devoted to the Great Outdoors, the Wonders of Nature and the haunting call of far-away places.

SCHOOL IDEALS (Sept. 1, 1958)
Poems and articles of Achievement, Loyalty, Courage, Opportunity and our great American heritage. A rural school note in the modern world.

IDEALS BINDER (holds 6 issues, no punching necessary) $3.00

And in addition—May we tell you about <u>*another*</u> *Ideals Publication?*

A Special Greeting Booklet

40 colorful pages
size 5⅜" by 7¼"
Cellophaned art cover

Christmas Greetings

only 50¢
with a colorful mailing envelope

This beautiful new Christmas greeting booklet has been prepared especially for you. Truly an exquisite — yet inexpensive — remembrance to send or to present to your loved ones at Christmas.

Most folks send CHRISTMAS GREETINGS just as they would a quality Christmas card — but Oh — how thrilled and delighted your friends will be with the artistic presentation of the true reverent spirit of Christmas — expressed on each lovely page.

CHRISTMAS GREETINGS — forty pages of inspiring poems of the season — reproductions of the finest Christmas art in full natural color — thoughts — and scriptural readings — will add depth and meaning to the rich experience of the Christmas message.

Send your orders to us TODAY! We will send CHRISTMAS GREETINGS direct to you promptly — or we will mail them to the folks you want to remember — identified as a gift from you — to arrive just before Christmas.

CHRISTMAS GREETINGS is not an issue in the regular series of IDEALS but must be ordered separately by all purchasers.

Costs no more than a quality Christmas Card